FARMERS CROSS

D1494008

BERNARD O'DONOGHUE

Farmers Cross

faber and faber

First published in 2011
by Faber and Faber Ltd
Bloomsbury House
74–77 Great Russell Street
London WC1B 3DA

Typeset by Faber and Faber Ltd
Printed in England by T. J. International Ltd, Padstow, Cornwall

A CIP record for this book
is available from the British Library

ISBN 978–0–571–26860–3

2 4 6 8 10 9 7 5 3 1

COMHAIRLE CHONTAE ÁTHA CLIATH THEAS
SOUTH DUBLIN COUNTY LIBRARIES

COUNTY LIBRARY, TOWN CENTRE, TALLAGHT
TO RENEW ANY ITEM TEL: 462 0073
OR ONLINE AT www.southdublinlibraries.ie

Items should be returned on or before the last date below. Fines, as displayed in the Library, will be charged on overdue items.

Acknowledgements

I am grateful to the editors of the following publications where some of these poems first appeared: *Agenda*, *Archipelago*, *Cork Literary Review*, *Irish Examiner*, *Irish Times*, *Keystone*, *London Review of Books*, *Manchester Poetry Review*, *Oxford Poetry*, *PN Review*, *Poetry Ireland Review*, *Poetry Review*, *Poetry Salzburg Review*, *The Reader*, *The SHOp*, *Smerilliana*, *Southword*, *The Spectator*, *Stand*, *Temenos*, *Times Literary Supplement*.

'City Planning' was written for *Urban Design Features*, eds. Malcolm Moor and Jon Rowland (Routledge, 2006). 'In Bavaria' is part of 'Chaff', printed by Oxford Poetry Broadsides in 2006. 'Ascent of Ben Bulben' was written to celebrate the Fiftieth Anniversary of the W. B. Yeats International Summer School, Sligo (2009), and printed as a broadsheet by The King Library Press, University of Kentucky, Lexington. 'Emigration' was published in *See How I Land: Oxford poets and exiled writers*, ed. Carole Angier (Heaventree Press, 2009). 'The Old Second Division' is published in *Burns and the Poets*, eds. Fiona Stafford and David Sergeant (Edinburgh University Press).

Contents

Bona-Fide Travellers 3
History 4
Freyfaxi 5
Vocation 6
Horses for Courses 7
Father Christmas 8
Tea Dolls 9
In Bavaria 10
Farmers Cross 11
Emigration 12
The Old Second Division 13
Geese Conversations 14
Crumpsall 15
The People through the Meadow
    Straying 16
Mere Planter and Fior-Ghael 18
Dockets 19
The Old Graveyard 20
Mirror 21
Lady's Smock 22
Aisling 23
Tinkers 24
Exhibitions 25
The Wanderer 26
Racho 30
Amicitia 31
Ascent of Ben Bulben 32
Virtue 34
Educated Flanagan 35

The Canon 36
Dream 37
Rubbish Theory 38
Flocks and Companies 39
Man of My Time 40
Tontine 41
City Planning 42
Penalty Points 44
Hover 45
Menagerie 46
The Worldwide Web 48
The Same Only Different 49
Casella 50
Dún an Óir 51
Dingle 52
Clegs at Totleigh Barton 53
Magic Lantern 54
The Year's Midnight 55

FARMERS CROSS

Of all the many places mentioned in poetry,
the exact location of most is not known for certain.
– BASHŌ, *Narrow Road to a Far Province*, 1689

Bona-Fide Travellers

It meant you had to be from somewhere else
to get a drink. But that was all right for us;
we always were, whether travelling west
or east. The trouble came when, dozing
on the boat, you half-came round and saw
the seabirds bathing, the gannet plunging
towards his bath, and battalions
of unknown children, speaking in accents
different from their parents. Your book
has slipped to the floor, the John Hinde postcard
has fallen out, and now you've lost your place.

In the real world, of course, there's no such person
as a Bona-Fide traveller. They will pull
the glass out of your hand and order you
to go back to the place you came from,
whatever you might have called that at the start.

History

Then they talked together until Dunstan spoke about St Edmund,
as Edmund's sword-bearer told the story to King Aethelstan, when
Dunstan was a young man and the sword-bearer was a very old man.
                    – AELFRIC's preface, *The Life of King Edmund*

Magie Din Beag, aged four in 1865,
was lifted on to her father's shoulders
at Abraham Lincoln's funeral.
Her father said to her: 'Never forget
that you were at Abraham Lincoln's funeral!'
He said it at the time, she told me, and again
at intervals throughout the rest of his life.
She told it to me in 1956
when I was ten, and said: 'Never forget
that you once knew an old woman
who had been at Abraham Lincoln's funeral
when she was four.' Fifty years ago now;
so what I say to you is: never forget
that you once read something by someone
who said they had known when they were young
someone who said their father told them
they had been to Abraham Lincoln's funeral.

Freyfaxi

No-one could touch her but Jer Mac himself,
the foxy mare, so the greatest honour
of my life was the day when he handed
across the reins and left me to guide her
to the yard, pulling her straining head up,
her haunches braced at forty-five degrees
to hold back the heavy float and haywynd.

Gunnar too would have fled Iceland, never
to return, but that his horse tripped in a hole
and threw him to the ground from where he gazed
in all directions at the shining meadows
and exclaimed aloud 'How beautiful it is!'
He could never leave it then; but it also meant
he'd chosen to remain where death closed in.

Vocation

Each cold October morning he went out
into the Gate Field and walked up and down,
like the horse-drawn seed-drill quartering every inch
to make sure the harvest was kept constant,
reading his Office, every Latin sentence
of the forty pages for the day. In the evening,
as the colder darkness fell with the crows'
harsh calling, he sat alone in the back
benches of the unheated chapel, hour
after hour, staring for inspiration
at the golden, unresponsive tabernacle.

Horses for Courses

When we went back, a horse was standing there.
Jer Mac, the greatest breaker of horses,
examined his teeth, judged his height in hands,
felt his fetlocks, pronounced himself satisfied:
'All right,' he said. 'Bring him in,' – which was of course
the start of all the trouble, as everyone knows.
Not long after, his wife was packed off back to her people,
and the child given to neighbours to be brought up.

Whatever they called it in Greek, our name for it
was *pisheogues*: those strange gifts that people,
neighbourly enemies, or gods, pushed through
railings and under wires, or hid in ditches
to confound us. We never discovered
exactly what gift it was that brought in its train
our father clutching his chest before he fell
and our particular wanderings across the seas.

Father Christmas

It was May or June when I first glimpsed him,
not far away: as ever, out of season,
either when the twilight thrush proclaims
unending summer, or when the guilty children
rummage through dark wardrobes for Christmas parcels,
in he blunders with his awful timing,
red suit pulled over his dustcoat any old how,
beard hooked crooked from his ears, and thrusting out
his dread portfolio of unnaturalised Greek terms:
aorta; cardiac; thrombosis. Or policemen's words
that make it all sound warranted:
stroke; violent; massive; laboured; and arrest.

Tea Dolls

On their icy trips up Greenland, everyone
took something, down to the two-year-old
who – herself perched on someone else's back –
carried a finger-measured puppet full of tea.
Viaticum would be the church's name for it:
essentials which you can't go on without.

I can't remember which of us took what
on the first flight to England, what small necessities
to live on, after Jer Mac improbably,
unprecedentedly, stubble-kissed us all,
me, male, and my two sisters, and said,
'Dia linn! I suppose we'll see them here no more.'

In Bavaria

Taketh the fruit, and let the chaff be still

— CHAUCER

The last morning, near the village shop,
I was pulled up short by a sudden smell
I hadn't breathed for years. Chaff: those mounds
that formed beneath the thresher, and remained
– a worthless, stifling quicksand – when the machine
had lolled out of the yard. You had to mind your step,
not knowing what your foot might strike against
after its short plunge through the yielding oat-floss.

On the way back to Munich, we stopped at Dachau.
It was closed on Monday, so we couldn't see
the full display of the commemorative centre.
But enough: mosquitoes menacing
umbrellas in the rain. The officers' blocks
behind the observation-turrets, still in place.
Half-grown grass and weeds along the line-side
where the first railway came to a stop.

Farmers Cross

My mother took to farming like a native,
as if she'd not grown up by city light;
she always said the front row in Heaven
would be filled exclusively by farmers.

She'd married into it. Then, as if things
were not bad enough, three days after he died
that cold March Sunday, a cheque he'd dated
on the day came back to us, explaining

'Not honoured: signatory deceased.'
His subscription to the *Irish Farmers Journal*.
But he hated farming: every uphill step
on the black hill where he'd been born and bred.

So she flew out for good and back to England,
from the new Airport near Cork, where the lights
fought a losing battle with the fog
at Farmers Cross. 'Why on Earth', everyone

was asking, 'build it on a hill? Why not keep
to lower ground east of the city? Wasn't it plain
to God it couldn't prosper there? That they'd
always said it was a hard farm to work.'

Emigration
for Yousif Qasmiyeh

Unhappy the man that keeps to the home place
and never finds time to escape to the city
where he can listen to the rain on the ceiling,
secure in the knowledge that it's causing no damage
to roof-thatch or haystack or anything of his.

Unhappy the man that never got up
on a tragic May morning, to go to the station
dressed out for America, where he might have stood
by the Statue of Liberty, or drunk in the light
that floods all the streets that converge on Times Square.

Unhappy the man that has lacked the occasion
to return to the village on a sun-struck May morning,
to shake the hands of the neighbours he'd left
a lifetime ago and tell the world's wonders,
before settling down by his hearth once again.

The Old Second Division

Before the days of Flymos, to cut the sloping lawn
above the lake in the Sixties state-of-the-art Business School
I held a rope supporting small Mr Howard
from Cowdenbeath (the old Scottish Second Division)
on a tight rein while he snipped the grass with shears.

He talked as he worked: for example about the time
when he was cycling along the Ring Road
at 3 a.m. one New Year's Day and suddenly felt
not so much drunk as very, very tired
so he laid his bike down and slept on the hard shoulder.

In the evening sometimes I went round
to his well-kept house in the suburbs
where he smoked Capstan, gave me a can
of McEwan's Export, and played me Beethoven
on the stereo he bought after his wife died.

Geese Conversations
i.m. Ian Niall

It would have been about this time of the year
that we watched the field-geese near Macroom
grow restless, preparing to call out
to the Canada geese flying overhead
to regions of thick-ribbëd ice, far away
from the Lee Scheme's kindly reclaimed stretches.

Crumpsall

At six o'clock she was woken by the noise
of boots on cobbles, walking to the mill:
that's what they said it was, though it sounded
like Jack Sweeney's working boots, tramping past
to the farm, hands behind his back,
careful not to glance in the window.

The hooter made her think of the brass whistle
Kate blew to summon him to the dinner.

At night she heard people laughing in the street,
where at home she'd hear the frantic barking
of dogs challenging each other or the Moon.
They were nice to her at school, most of the time,
but there were so many things they didn't know:
butter-boxes, milk-tanks, cocks of hay,
the collar and hames around the horse's neck,
or people calling 'How!' to the cows coming in for milking.

So when could she go home, and lie in her own bed
thinking back to work-sirens and trains.

The People through the Meadow Straying
Piers Plowman: Prologue

In the season of summer   with the sun at its highest
I dressed in my work-clothes   like any poor shepherd,
in the garb of a hermit   but for worldly work
and set off through the country   to find what I'd find.
I met many wonders   and uncommon sights,
till one morning in May   on the hills behind Malvern
I fell sound asleep,   worn out by the walking.
As I lay on the ground,   resting and slumbering,
I'd this marvellous dream   I'll describe to you now.
I saw all the good   that live in the world
and the bad just as busy,   be certain of that:
loyalty, betrayal,   let-down and cunning –
I saw them all in my sleep: that's what I'm saying.
I looked to the East,   in the track of the sun
and saw a great tower –   Truth's home, I imagined.
Then to the westward   I looked shortly after
and saw a deep valley.   Death lived down there,
I'd no doubt in my mind,   with all evil spirits.
I saw in the middle   between these two points
a beautiful meadow,   thronging with people
of every station,   the poor and the needful
who slaved at their labours   as this hard world requires them.
Some trudged behind ploughs   with no chance of a respite,
sowing and seeding.   They worked without ceasing
to win for the people   what the greedy would waste.
Others grew proud   and dressed up accordingly,
their faces and get-up   a sight for sore eyes.
But many more,   it has to be said,
lived in penance and prayer   for the love of Our Lord,

in the confident hope   of ascending to Heaven.
As monks and nuns   they remained in their cells,
never wishing   to dash round the country
on the lookout for luxuries   to pamper their whims.
Some took to business   and did very well –
at least as we see it –   'getting on in the world'.
More had a fine time,   acting the clown
With dancing and singing   and swearing their heads off,
inventing daft stories,   making fools of themselves.
Such people imagine   that work's a poor option.

Mere Planter and Fior-Ghael
for Tadhg Foley

Jack Sweeney had been injured at Verdun
and revered British virtues. My father said
he'd turn up the volume on *Housewives' Choice*
if ever 'Land of Hope and Glory' coincided
with Jack walking past to work at Mac's.
Jer Mac wanted the Germans to win the war,
grunting assent to Lord Haw Haw's taunts.
But Jack revered him too, a tasty farmer

who planted rows of sycamore and ash
along the passage to his yard. Every May,
Jack and Phil Micheál marched out with pikes
over their shoulders to spend a week trimming
the long hedge with slashers, shaping an avenue
that would have graced the drive to any big house.
Like that public servant with an Irish name,
who died in a lonely copse-edge near Abingdon.

Dockets

and this, your all-licens'd fool

Although it's hard to think what he would buy
requiring a receipt – his needs being met
by the cluster of silver and copper pushed
along the counter for the next pint and half-one –
when he was found a few days dead in the house
he'd squatted in with dogs for thirty years,
there was a neat pile of dockets from the creamery store
held in place by the red inner stone
of a pre-electric iron. Proof of what?
That his life was ordered in its way:
exactly how much to drink, in what proportions,
to go home happy, and yet able to get up
and stalk past reproachful windows, eyes ahead,
and spend the day painting from a ladder?

In a different life, might he have been
Jimmy the Clerk, in jacket and red tie,
carrying the neat brown attaché case
to the Stations for the priest, and snapping
it open on the kitchen table, disguised for Mass
beneath the candles and starched white linen cloth,
to reveal the vessels of the Sacrament:
ciborium, amice, maniple and stole?

The Old Graveyard

It still commands the best view from the village,
across the unkempt pitch-and-putt course
to the river. The stone wall, perfectly jointed
at the corners, was built – or so they say –
by Dan Hugh, the mason-poet, from the ruins
of the Benedictine church that dated from
the seventh century. To read inscriptions
the Americans spray shaving-foam, trying
to bring to light the names of ancestors.
In autumn when they've gone back to resume
their duties in New England or Chicago,
the cosmetic blear still discolours the stone.

Mirror

for Tom and Douglas Paulin

On the mantelpiece, facing the picture window
which frames the saint's island by Narin Strand,
there's that darkening piece of paper with its text
that guardedly catches happiness and its
components – of all things the hardest
to set down and, once set down,
the hardest to keep bright. *You've made a table*
you say, and are happy. As once I was,
having made a rough milking-stool with wood
left over from the measuring of Mick Mac,
or as Tom joined his lines together
from moments, thoughts, and salt-sea island views
that are not easy to assemble if
they're not already there by the ticking clock.

Lady's Smock

Past the odour-of-sanctity primroses
in their tight nests of wrinkle-green
by the well, and the violets,
hardly daring to breathe, on the ditch
above them. On to the wet fields
and the wiry filigree below
the girl's-dress mauve elegance
of this flower, rooted amid rush-spires,
just come out at the start of a new season.

Aisling

My dreams now increasingly move along
the unmetalled roads of childhood: sometimes
I'm already on them before I fall fully asleep,
watching the camber edging round the corner.

But often too I dream of a wrecked room,
unreclaimed when the old house was done up.
There's mould on everything, and grass
invading from the broken chutes outside.

My clear duty is every time the same:
to clean it out, ready for the nextcomers.
But then something intervenes to mean
I don't need to prepare it after all.

And then I am back out on the roads again,
at the turn by Julia's well, or further down
by Dan Jim's boreen, by the primrose stream
that Dominic dammed to make pools for his cows:

where I once really met a tinker couple
trudging through the rain ahead of me.
No matter how slow I walked, I couldn't fail
to overtake them, when they stood and watched

a donkey grazing by the verge, a ravelled rope
around his neck. The woman drew her shawl aside,
showing her face, and questioned me directly:
'Do you know is anyone the own of him?'

Tinkers

A dog's obeyed in office

I feared them like I also feared the Guards
as wielders of some undomestic power,
afraid that, if I didn't make out well,
I'd end up in a tent beside the road,
unable to get warm: that, when I'd gone,
all I'd leave behind would be a patch
of grey, wet ash where the green sycamore
had offered little light or sweetness.

In later years, of course, I came to know
that their authority was nothing to be afraid of:
that the weak are always stigmatised
to make things even better for the strong.

And yet beware! Remember that young boy
who quarrelled over butter at our door
and took his vengeance by winning over
the dog the family had set on him.
The dog stood spellbound, listening, ears alert,
to the hoarse, alluring voice calling 'Bran! Bran!'

Exhibitions
for Morag Morris

On the way back from the dentist, I still stop
at the Art Gallery to view the same canvases
I've seen year after year: the forest fire
with its cows reassuringly indifferent,
Pissarro's dotted suburbs, St Catherine
with her lilies. The attendant tells me, once again,
that many of their best holdings stay
in the cellar, never to see the light.

At home there's no space left on the walls
to hang the new pictures I'd like to introduce.
I move things round, hopelessly: the icon
of the virgin is now over the stairs,
her matt, pastel gaze reproving us,
which before caught the light from the fire.

The Wanderer

i.m. Gerard Hermele and Margaret Wilkinson

It's true that when you are depressed
you can be raised by the mercy
of God, however bad things seem,
however far it seems that you have strayed
from the fields of home, as you stand
smoking by the rail and watching
the big waves hitting against the dark.
But there's no cure for it.

This is how the exile put it –
refugee rather, when he thought
of those terrible, death-filled months:
'How often have I woken up
to feel the weight still unlifted
by the dawn chorus. And I don't dare
change the medicine, or go back
to the doctor in case he tells me
"pull yourself together". Oh I know
it's the thing to do, to pretend
there's nothing wrong, however bad
you feel. That's all very well;
but your low spirits can't take
much more, and shouting doesn't help.
I am sure this is why
people with a bit of ambition
often have to bottle it all up
in quiet desperation:
just as I myself, in a desperate state,
years from home and friends,
and sick with misery,

must chain my wretched tongue
as I watch them burying
my dear friends in the cold earth.
I've gone anywhere since,
attempting to find anyone
to talk to me or give me a roof
over my head or something
to turn my hand to. If you've been through it,
you know what a poor companion grief is
if you've not a friend in the world.
You think about pilgrimage, not money:
how your heart's seized up, not about getting on
in the world. You remember friends,
how kind they were: the people who gave you money
when you were small. All joys now gone.

   Whoever lacks advice from any quarter
knows this well. Sleep and sorrow
are never parted, holding down
the man that lives on his own.
Dreaming, he thinks he shakes the hand
of his neighbour: that he sits beside him
on a fireside bench, just like the old days,
listening to whatever was on the radio.
Then he wakes up again, alone;
the fire's gone out, and he sees at his feet
the grey ash, listening to the crows protesting
from the windblown pine-screen,
while the squall rages, with a touch of sleet.

   That's when he feels his loneliness most,
the longing for friends. He tries to imagine
they're there in the room with him,
laughing and talking. He talks back,
peering at their faces. But no one's there;

the travelling spirits fade into the corner,
without a word. The sorrow is back
when friends can only be found
in a failing memory.

So what I can't understand is why on earth
I don't completely give up on it all
when I think of the end of everyone's days,
and how they all have left the arena,
the strong and the good. In the same way
this precious earth weakens a fraction
each passing day: something that only
the aged man appreciates fully.
You have to be patient: not too impetuous
in thought or in word; not cowardly,
but not violent either. Don't flinch,
but don't press your own case.
Don't be greedy, and don't start boasting
until you're sure what you can achieve.
When you start holding forth, be sure you know
exactly what your drift is and where it will end.
Any person with a spark of sense
must know by now how desperate it will be
when the whole of our dear world
stands silent and empty. Already in places
they've had to abandon traditional fields
where the ground has dried out or the oil is used up.
Cities lie in ruins; populations lie dead,
their bodies heaped by the crumbling walls.
Some die in battle, but more are victims
of assault from the skies. Some are left
for scavengers to come under cover of night
to steal what they can. Few have the honour

of dignified burial by friend or relation.
Whatever it was brought the world into being
reverses the process till all is a void.

    The person who has grasped the order of things
and fully understands the depth of this tragedy,
has time to reflect on the endless conflicts
and lament for the future. "Where have machines gone?
Where are the drivers? What has become
Of friendship and holiday?
Alas for the paintings! Alas for cathedrals
and the places where people were happy together!
It has all passed away to the depths of the dark
as if it never had been. Now in their place
there's a desert of tar with hardly a trace
of the lines on the map where once there were streets.
The bombs have won out,
achieving their ends; the driver's
a mummy, congealed in his seat.
So much for him! The wind whirls around
sanddrifts or snowdrifts, depending on where.
Winter triumphant, too cold or too hot
as the north moves south, destroying all growth.
Everything's hard in the state of the world,
changed for the worse by the rule of the heavens.
Riches won't last and neither will friendship.
Man least of all – his relations all gone.
Everything on earth will shudder and die."'

    That's what he said, this solitary wise man.
It's good to keep faith, and not to reveal
the fear in your heart if you can't see a way
of making things better. All you can do
is to place your trust in the god in the heavens
where alone is stability, if it is found anywhere.

Racho

So strange and individual, I'm not quite sure
I'm not making it up. Could it be true:
that he spent a night in Spenser's castle
at Kilcolman, warmed by a fire of coals
brought in a bucket by the local farmer
(the same farmer who put up a double row
of electric fencing to keep the scholars out)?

'Marek' or 'Marius' or sometimes 'Mark',
all depending on how Polish he felt
or how epicurean. He saw so shrewdly
the poor follies of poets: self-revealing,
self-promoting, self-anything. They had to write
to the A level examiners apologising
for his paper's elegant brutalities.

He did exist: at least, as I found out later,
he had existed. I met a woman
at a grand dinner, whose son had known him
at school, and who told me he'd died young:
not, as I had often speculated,
by suicide, but of commonplace cancer
through which any ordinary body might have failed.

Amicitia

When Dante's life-and-death love Beatrice,
his grace-conferring lady, died, they sought
to stanch his grief by marrying him
to Gemma Donati, his close friend's kinswoman.
But – the story goes – he was not comforted,
even after the birth of their four children,
forbidding her to visit him in exile.

Yes, we know these tales of unrequited love
and lifelong hang-ups. And we also know
what truth they have. A guess based on ourselves
is more persuasive: that he kept in touch
through friends and relatives; that he wrote to her,
saying how wearisome it is to climb
unfriendly stairs, and how salt-bitter the taste

of food prepared by other hands. And that
the memory that had the sweetest poignancy
was themselves, young, going out at student weekends
to eye the talent along the Ponte Vecchio.

Ascent of Ben Bulben

i.m. George Watson

*so rare a thing is absolute congeniality in every attitude
and habit even among dear friends*
— PETRARCH

There are two ways of climbing to the summit
of Ben Bulben: one behind Drumcliff churchyard,
east at the creamery and up the hill.
There you pass elegant retirement houses
on ever-narrowing woodbine-scented roads,
until you have to leave the car and walk,
straight up the formidable, striated front.

This is a hard way. If you make it,
look back down at all that you have left:
the sea stretching from the Rosses to the foot
of Knocknarea – seeing maybe the last thing
that Diarmuid saw before his death:
the unexcavated cairn of the fierce queen
who scorns the dangerous currents at Strandhill.

The other way is easier: you ask Jimmy Waters
whose business visits to the local farms
have taught him every yard and forest-track
where the mountain-stream disappears under
the ground. He'll tell you which warnings to ignore:
the gates you can open, and what bogs
above Glencar you can still take in your stride.

And the Yeatses: which way for them? Did they stand
and clap their hands to send the swans wheeling
in broken rings, over the sea and across
to the other mountain, to wonder at the gist
of what they mean? Or did they watch the races
being set up on the yellow strand,
where men still break stones on the road below?

Virtue

He had been unfaithful once, unlikely
as that seemed when, silver-haired and blind,
he let her lead him up the aisle each Sunday.
Some Jezebel, the story was, had lured him
off to Blackpool one weekend, long in the past.
I went along to Mass when I came home,
and enjoyed hearing the praise on every side
of such an exemplary grandnephew.
After he died, she moved to sheltered housing
somewhere near Parbold in the scenic north
of Lancashire, but we sometimes still went
to take her to Mass, tearfully sniffing
into her scented hankie, recalling Stuart
and how she missed his arm upon her shoulder.

Educated Flanagan

Educated Flanagan had books to beat the band,
and he carried them around in cardboard boxes,
more dog-eared every year, from site to site,
like our poor dog, moving her pups by mouth
till every last one of them was dead. At weekends
he would lie, free from the trench's drudgery
(*'The shovel, Educated! Christ, you're dreaming!'*),
losing himself in any fact or fiction,
in forum, field or fane. Where did it start?
A Christian Brother, or a spoilt priest
who realised he had no vocation?
Or just a man who by some electric pulse
tuned in across the centuries to find
the wavelength for Homer and the Golden Legend.

The Canon

An ascetic: but was he before his time
or after it? He would only eat
wholemeal bread and an egg boiled for precisely
three-and-a-half minutes. A music man,
he laid his white and slender sacerdotal
finger along his cheek, meeting the steel
of his uniquely short-cut hair, to concentrate
on the slow movement, then waved it all away
as the violin relaxed into the rondo
that the rest of us had been waiting to jig along to.

Dream

In a wheelchair, just inside the door,
you looked even older and frailer,
winding your handkerchief around your wrist
as usual. I stole past, thinking
you wouldn't notice me. But you had seen:
your hand was now on my arm and, smiling,
you addressed me by someone else's name.
So I asked how you were feeling, and you said,
as you'd always said, 'Better than I should
at this stage of my life.' And smiled again.

Rubbish Theory
i.m. Dinny Hickey

You must stop me if I've told you this before:
but the rule is that things must first pass through
a season of neglect during which they're thrown out
as rubbish, in order to become scarce enough
to be worth collecting – like Dinny's sayings
and his seed-drill that now is rotting
beneath the foliage in our front yard.

By now both have served their death-apprenticeship
of years unvalued, so it's time to try
recycling: *'first in a wood, last in a bog.'*
'Setting spuds for Jer Mac with Thade Buckley
    from Doon.'
Still folly as yet maybe; but take note
that the young trees around us in their turn
are already becoming history;

the man who planted our mountain ash,
hacking through frozen pencil one cold March,
is now buried himself in New South Wales;
Ted's apple trees are learning to resist
the plundering of the bullfinches in spring
and soon, no doubt, they'll crop. So what time
is this? A time to mourn or a time to sing?

Flocks and Companies

At first I thought the birds were singletons
like the fox was: the cuckoo; the corncrake.
But then I learned that they, like all of us,
lived in societies, and that the wren
who trilled within my hearing yesterday
was one of many. Now I'm not sure again,
listening to the mistle thrush outside my room,
always the same song, always the same branch:
or woken every morning by the starling
who's sung the same foreboding sequence
since February – *'time to go, I told you so'* –
too much mind of his own for one of the crowd.
But I saw what he was sent for, what he was warning,
when the first ordnance descended on Fallujah.

Man of My Time
after Quasimodo

Still the same old exponent of sling and stone,
man of my time. You stood by the mainmast
as the Furies' wings, at death's zenith, beat overhead.

You've seen it all – the burnt jeeps by Basra,
the gallows, the rack, the wheel of torture. You
have looked on, your precise learning geared
to extermination, loveless, Christless.
You've gone on killing, as your forefathers killed,
and the animals that saw them for the first time, killed.
And this blood smells the same as on the day
when brother first said to brother 'Let us walk
in the fields'. His echo, cold and decided,
rings clear to your day.
                        Sons, put from your mind
the clouds of blood that have rained down on the earth.
Forget your fathers: their tombs are filled with ash,
their hearts embalmed by Black Wings and the wind.

Tontine

i.m. Michael Donaghy

Survivor takes all, we reflect,
standing together in the rain
outside the crematorium
under the heron's raucous boom
as the crows mob him overhead.

City Planning
for Marie-José and Malcolm Moor

Looked down on from the tower-top, it's fields
by other means: the street's the headland
where the mown hay has to be pulled back
making room for the tractor's clumsy, ribbed
back wheel. The Cathedrals, both persuasions,
face each other out across the skyline,
two swollen ricks, one of wheat, one barley.

So we, God's caretakers, are at liberty
to reshape it or to knock it all back down
and start again: to cut corners; leave fallow
the ground which only last year was (say)
the fruitful Eden where the Euphrates meets
the Tigris: to rub out the olive-drills
and rows of lights, the wide wrinkles of night life.

And we're entitled too to smooth away
rough features, to erase them from the air
just as we'd brush the hair out of someone's eyes.
We make straight lines, arcing out from the centre,
just as in the old days we would level
a fence between two fields and bulldoze it
into the quarry, covering the prehistoric stone.

But you must have seen those maps, photographed
from space – how the city's light shows up
by infrared, and how the dark stays dark,
asleep at the edges. And those aerial pictures
of ring-forts, how their subcutaneous veins
show through the earth's temporal covering
which has been hurriedly slung over them.

Penalty Points

A reasonable system: after three years
the mark of crime's expunged, just like when
the punishment due to sin fades away
in the brief millennia of Purgatory.

You write to the Chief Constable, pleading
absent-mindedness, or a pressing engagement
further along the road: a matter possibly
of life and death. But none of it's any good:

they send it back endorsed, like the mark of Cain
stamped upon your forehead, or like the taste
of guilt that stays inexplicably in your mind
in the first anxious seconds after waking.

Hover

for John O'Donoghue

After our sighting of the kingfisher,
humming straight up the river in its path
of turquoise, we would stop at the bridge
several times a day, hoping and praying.
We saw the dipper, now a bird as common
as the blackbird, corncrake or the crane;
often we'd see the heron keeping an eye
on its schedule, before lifting off
into the wind and swinging in a big arc
towards Cullen with the wind to its back.

But shortly before we left, among the rocks
beneath the outlaw's cave, we caught a still
rarer glimpse: the otter, briefly incautious,
appearing in the sun, then gone. And now
it was him we went back to look for.
We didn't see him again. But we've marked
the rock he paused on, so we'll return
next year and find him, sure of the place
above the water where his holt is, dark
and sheltered from the bandogs of the day.

Menagerie

The ochre-coloured farmhouse at Gort Athaig
doesn't need much enhancing; but there's a story too.
At right angles to it, there's a wall: crude enough,
of breeze blocks half-whitewashed so the grey lines
show through. A group of visiting students
offered once to make a mural there, and did:
they painted tigers, lions, a giraffe,
and a bright troupe of circus horses. For years
the beasts guarded that turn that keeps away
tourist buses that can't fit around the corner.

In that wild-weathered place, overlooking
the finest landscape in the whole of Beara,
they lost their vividness in the course of time
until finally, preparing for the Stations,
they covered them with grey swathes of whitewash
(you know how marvellously it dries like snow).

The next April, Fossett's Circus – a thrilling mile
of trucks and caravans – came trundling out
of Castletownbere to set up in Killarney.
They missed the direct road to Eyeries,
and set off past Cahermore, over the Atlantic,
past Bernie's radio-mast and the coppermines
at Allihies. On they laboured, ten miles an hour,
gathering behind them an impatient line
of late-working tractors, vets, and dance-goers,

until they came to the wall at Claonach corner.
They couldn't get around; they couldn't turn back,
so painfully they uncoupled the wagons,
one by one, and overnight they penned
the animals in the sloping corner field.

Next morning, 6 a.m., the owner of
the ochre house was driving back late
from a protracted wedding celebration,
and, turning round the last bend for home,
saw them before her: returned from the wall,
escaped from their painted frame,
grazing in Gort Athaig above the sea.

The Worldwide Web

Tom

In jail I would befriend
the prison dog and look
through his unblinking eyes
past his interpretative cones,
secure in the knowledge that
the line continues,
as by e-mail, to emerge
through some other dog's eyes
which might find yours
reaching out in turn at home.

The Same Only Different

to Ellie

It's different, I know: you broke your ankle
at a wedding, tripping over a tent-peg.
But still, as you wade on crutches towards me
along the wet pavement through the shadows,
beaming and calling, you are the same
as the ten-month-old child who plunged,
reckless and generous, towards outstretched hands,
risking all on the tiles of the kitchen floor.

Casella

DANTE, *Purgatorio ii, 61–81*

Virgil said 'I think you must believe
that we know all about arrangements here;
but we are outsiders, just the same as you are.

'We'd only just arrived here before you,
but by so rough and arduous a route
that the climb will seem as nothing from here on.'

The spirits who had spotted by my breathing
that I was still alive, were so astonished
that they all turned pale; and, just the way

a crowd will gather to hear the latest news
from a messenger carrying the olive branch,
and no one cares if they trample on each other,

so these spirits, forgetting their higher purpose,
all jostled for a good view of my face,
distracted from the path towards perfection.

Then I saw one of them push right to the front
to hug me with such particular affection
that he inspired me to do the same to him.

Ah shadows, with substance only on the surface!
Three times my arms closed up behind him,
and passed straight through him, back on to my chest.

Dún an Óir

It is always quarter-to-six
around these beaches, time
to be heading home. Call back
the children and shake out the rugs.
Give up for lost the items buried
in the sand: miniature rakes
and shells and summer arguments.

Dingle

i.m. Garry MacMahon

They'd promised a fine summer from the start:
the dolphins, they said, had shoaled into the bay
in April, and the warblers came a full week
earlier than usual. So we lay on twin beds
in the Gaeltacht digs, reading novels,
eating oranges and waiting for the rain
to stop so that we'd be able to walk again
above the sea by Ballydavid. But as we stood,
seeking out formulas and metaphors
for how the dashed spray poured back down
into the depths off the faces of the gravestone-granite
rocks, something changed. And the next morning
we read in the local paper that the dolphins
had unexpectedly gone back out to sea.

Clegs at Totleigh Barton

Plenty of gates to lean on around here,
and plenty of time to watch the horse-flies
on the dung, to see if they are really
generated from it. There is more chill
than blessing in this gentle breeze off Dartmoor,
more edge than you'd expect in late September.
So: winter soon, after no summer.

Yes, this is the place: 'Road liable to flooding'.
This is where Grace Ingoldby did handstands
on the frosty tarmac. Where Mick Imlah stayed,
when we nearly ran over the cliff
at Morwenstow, looking for Hawker's hut
in which the old man composed, or didn't.

Before Grace's son died in the fire, and Grace died too.
Before Mick got ill. Today I am back on my own
to stare at these insects at their dreadful trade.

'Now try your brakes', it still says on the sign.

Magic Lantern

A swallow of the dead, a bat got in
and beat on the bedroom wall. One winter
a comet, like an old-style, opened-out
girl's hairgrip, was framed for nights. But stranger
than any portent, and more regular,
as they walked up the back path from milking,
the bucket's glint cast a bent line of light
that moved along the wall, beginning at
the top right-hand corner, and panning southwards,
every blessed sunlit summer's morning.

The Year's Midnight

Andrew Glyn, 22 December 2007

We watched the mornings lighten, till the day
when the bus would at last appear with its lights
switched off. We speculated idly why it was
that the days lengthened first towards the evening
and later in the morning, half-recalling that it had
something to do with the angle of the earth
upon its axis. There were other signs of progress:

the winter robin gradually joined
by the tentative and wistful mistle thrush.
I threw in Timmy Buckley's age-old wisdom:
'Light until six o'clock the first of February'.
And we waited for the leaves to cover over
the exposed ruins of last April's nests
in the tall trees at the summit of South Park.

Then, when you became ill, it all grew
academic. The bus's lights; travelling forth
without a coat; the birds about their business.
But it was as predictable as the seasons
that you would die on the shortest day,
a day when the world was least enlightened
and the shades fell not long after 3 p.m.